Social media marketing guide for facebook advertising.

Create your business, develop your strategies and sell your brand.

JOAN SMITH

Table of Contents

BOOK DESCRIPTION.. 8

INTRODUCTION... 9

CHAPTER 1: SOCIAL MEDIA MARKETING................... 12

1.1　Why Facebook...12

1.2　Facebook Advertising and Vocabulary..................16

1.3　Campaigning, Ad Sets, The Ad................................19

2.1　1.4 Facebook Business Manager.............................22

CHAPTER 2: CREATE YOUR STRATEGIES................... 24

2.1 Develop your Strategies...24

2.2 Advertising Strategies on Facebook..........................29

2.3 What is Facebook Marketing..30

Reasons to Start Advertising on Facebook Right Now31

2.4 What are the Means of doing Facebook Marketing34
　Messenger 34
　Comments..37
　Collecting Positive Reviews..39
　Consumer Generated Content.......................................43

CHAPTER 3: CREATING YOUR BUSINESS PAGE....... 48

3.1 Account and Homepage: Defining your Brand...........48

3.2 Keyword Selection 49

Use descriptive keywords in the "About" section.. 49

3.3 Optimizing your Page **49**
Choose a username that is meaningful and memorable 50
Optimize the images on your page 50
Pinned posts 51

3.4 Post, Content, Images, Video, Posting link **52**
Images 52
Get A Logo and Cover Art Made 54
Creating an Attractive Profile 55
Where to Find Images for Posting 56
Videos 56

3.5 Optimizing posting time **58**

CHAPTER 4: CREATING AUDIENCE LIST FOR FACEBOOK ADS 61

4.1 How to create an Audience List **61**

4.2 Understanding the Marketing Objective **66**

4.3 How to increase Visibility on your Post **67**

CHAPTER 5: INSTALL FACEBOOK PIXEL 70
A Guide on Using Facebook Pixels 72
Facebook Pixel's 17 Standard Events 73
Facebook Pixel's Custom Events 75
Once this is done, the next thing you should do is to select a category and click 'Next'. 75
Split Standard events with Custom Conversions 76
Creating Facebook Pixels to Add to your Website ... 76
Wait for a moment for your pixel to be created then click on 'Set up the Pixel Now'. 77

CHAPTER 6: FACEBOOK RETARGETING 79

6.1 How to use Facebook Retargeting..................................79

6.2 How to creating a retargeting Campaign on Facebook..81

CHAPTER 7: CREATING A FACEBOOK AD CAMPAIGN: HOW TO BE SUCCESSFUL..85

7.1 The sales conversion process..................................85

7.2 Promoting page posts..86

7.3 Getting more links and click to your website....87

7.4 Defining and Understanding your Audience.............88

7.5 Profit from remarketing on Facebook........................89
   Gain followers with Facebook Remarketing Lists....89
   Remarket to those that are Already Following your Page..91
   Use Facebook Targeting Options to Layer your Custom Audiences..91
   Keep your Goals in Mind when Scheduling your Ads 93
   Use Lookalike Customers to Layer new Customers into your Custom Audience..93
   Take Advantage of the Window of Opportunity...........94

CHAPTER 8: FACEBOOK ALGORITHM...........................97

CHAPTER 9: HOW TO MONITORING YOUR FACEBOOK RESULT...101
   Reading Metrics...102

CHAPTER 10: FACEBOOK ADS AND GDPR COMPLIANCE..107

AdWords vs. Facebook...107

The Definition of the Goals 109

Facebook Leads: How to Get Quality Leads 113

GDPR Compliance 114

CONCLUSION 117

Text Copyright © [Joan Smith]

All rights reserved. No part of this guide may be reproduced in any form without permission in writing from the publisher except in the case of brief quotations embodied in critical articles or reviews.

Legal & Disclaimer

The information contained in this book and its contents is not designed to replace or take the place of any form of medical or professional advice; and is not meant to replace the need for independent medical, financial, legal or other professional advice or services, as may be required. The content and information in this book has been provided for educational and entertainment purposes only.

The content and information contained in this book has been compiled from sources deemed reliable, and it is accurate to the best of the Author's knowledge, information and belief. However, the Author cannot guarantee its accuracy and validity and cannot be held liable for any errors and/or omissions. Further, changes are periodically made to this book as and when needed. Where appropriate and/or necessary, you must consult a professional (including but not limited to your doctor, attorney, financial advisor or such other professional advisor) before using any of the suggested remedies, techniques, or information in this book.

Upon using the contents and information contained in this book, you agree to hold harmless the Author from and against any damages, costs, and expenses, including any legal fees potentially resulting from the application of any of the information provided by this book. This disclaimer applies to any loss, damages or injury caused by the use and application, whether directly or indirectly, of any advice or information presented, whether for breach of contract, tort, negligence, personal injury, criminal intent, or under any other cause of action.

You agree to accept all risks of using the information presented inside this book.

You agree that by continuing to read this book, where appropriate and/or necessary, you shall consult a professional (including but not limited to your doctor, attorney, or financial advisor or such other advisor as needed) before using any of the suggested remedies, techniques, or information in this book.

Book Description

If you want to reach your audience effectively, you **need** to have Facebook.

You need to be advertising on this platform if you aren't already doing so. Regardless of your campaign goals, Facebook Insights is designed to help you meet that goal. At first glance, the world of Facebook advertisements can seem like an incredibly complex world. Added to that is the uncertainty that you feel, not knowing if your ad is going to be successful or not.

If your brand is not already leveraging on the advantages of Facebook advertising, then your brand is missing out. Here is why your business is on the losing end if you are not tapping into the potential of what Facebook has to offer:

Approximately 80% of all Internet users are on Facebook. What this translates to is that a lot of your customers are going to be spending their time on Facebook. The social media platform has 1.85 billion users alone, and most of these users are likely to log into the platform several times a day. It doesn't matter who your customers are, or where they're located in the world, the only thing that matters to your brand and business is that they are on Facebook. You should be on it too because of that fact.

INTRODUCTION

Facebook is probably one of the most recognizable social media platforms out there.

It is practically everywhere that we go. From our favorite coffee shops which encourage us to connect with them on their Facebook profile, to new company sign-ups which make it easy to create a new account by simply connecting our Facebook profiles, Facebook has become a significant part of our daily lives.
This social media site has been around since 2004. However, Facebook advertising only started to really gain momentum in 2014.
They believed in keeping their news feed exclusively for content from friends and family.
How many things have changed since then?

Today, it is impossible to scroll through our newsfeed without seeing at least a couple of ads along the way. It was in 2013 when a change was slowly starting to happen.

It was around that time that ads slowly started appearing on the news feed of a Facebook user. It was then that the rise of social advertising was just starting to begin.

What made Facebook different from a lot of other social media sites was that they could target their ads towards the right groups of audiences based on years of detail which they had accumulated over time. Data could come from something as simple as the content that they users like, what they might have commented on in the past, or even content which was previously shared.

Chapter 1: Social Media Marketing

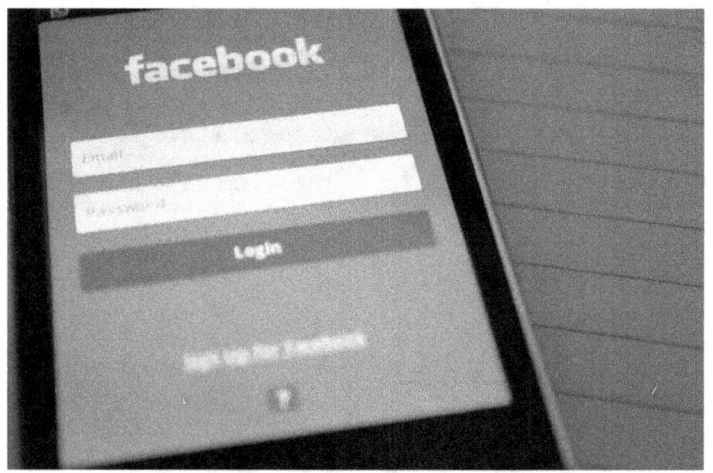

1.1 Why Facebook

• MARKETERS CANNOT DENY THAT:

Facebook is one of the emerging giants in the advertising world. Almost every business that is targeted to users of this day and age has a Facebook Page.
Facebook has helped businesses grow in their reach, build a loyal customer base, and generate sales. Businesses advertising on Facebook are recently over three million and it looks like this trend will stick for a while. Before joining millions of businesses worldwide on their advertising efforts on Facebook, here is what you need to know about this social media platform.

• YOUR AUDIENCE MOST CERTAINLY ON IT

Daily active users on Facebook are currently more than 1.13 billion. Those who use mobile devices to access Facebook is more than 1.03 billion. Its user amounts to the entire population of China. This means that your target audience, no matter their demographics, are very likely on it - almost every day.

• YOUR AUDIENCE IS LOOKING AT IT

On average, users spend up to 50 minutes a day on social media platforms - be it Facebook, Instagram, Twitter, or Messenger. This means that in the duration that they are using Facebook; they are highly likely to come across advertisements that convert them to customers. This gives you time to reach out to them through your ad campaigns.

• IT HELPS YOU TARGET YOUR AUDIENCE

Facebook allows businesses to target their audience through behavior, interests, age, gender, demographics, location, and more. This helps you ensure that your ad is going to the right people at the right time and will eventually convert them to become your paying customers.

• ORGANIC REACH IS ON THE DECLINE

In the past few years, organic reach on Facebook has been on a decline and almost hit zero. This is due to more ad content competing for News Feed space. What this means for advertisers is that it is hard to appear on users' News Feed even if they are already following you, as paying advertisers are competing for that space. Not only that, once you are out, you are out. It is near impossible to passively get back on your followers' radar unless you pay to do so.

• GAIN CONNECTIONS

With Facebook ads, the best thing that you can do is advertising your page. This gives you new followers. You will also determine those who enjoy Facebook and are within your target when they click your advertisements. People will get to know your organization, services, products, and yourself more when you connect them on your Fan Page. Use the Insights features to collect some data about your Page's performance before you put up your ad. How many new likes do you get weekly? What is your current demographic? This helps you craft a more effective and targeted campaign.

• ACQUIRE LEADS

Your goal with advertising on Facebook should be to acquire leads. What would you want them to do as a result of engaging with your ad? Maybe you want your potential leads to sign up for your monthly newsletter. In this case, you need to create your ad in a way that it sends users to your website where they can sign up. Make sure that the call to action is clear so that it is easy for your audience to understand what they are being led to do. Think of the user journey and try to make it as seamless and fuss-free as possible. If your intention for the advertisement is to have your audience be aware of you, put your contact number and address so they do not necessarily have to click on the advertisement to contact you. Fit in as many details as you can in the 90 characters that you have in the body of the ad.

- ## RECONNECT WITH YOUR COMMUNITY

Sponsored stories and Promoted posts enable you to reconnect with your current community and interact with dormant fans. As mentioned earlier, when you drop out of the News Feed of your fans, it can be very difficult to get back into that News Feed organically, and you may have to use some advertising funds to reconnect with them. Sponsored stories can help you target the people who have connected to your Page. Sponsored story ad will appear in the right sidebar of Facebook pages. The Promoted post option can be used to push posts directly into the News Feeds of fans who otherwise may not see it.

1.2 Facebook Advertising and Vocabulary

Just like every other social media platform, Facebook has evolved to meet the demands of businesses and marketers in today's digital age. Facebook offers several types of ads for marketers to choose from depending on what their business goals or needs may be.

Let's take a look at some of the various types of sponsored content and ads which you will commonly come across on the social media site:

- SPONSORED CONTENT:

    One of the most common content types available on the platform, sponsored stories involves content which has been created based on the consumer's interaction with a specific brand. These types of content function in a similar way to organic stories, whereby only the users Facebook friends will be able to see the content of this ad. With sponsored stories, brands will be able to adjust their targets accordingly based on gender, location, age, and other important demographic details to help them better target the correct group of audiences.

- **SPONSORED ADS:**

  Sponsored stories are created by marketers of the brand. It is the marketer who is in control of the content and the audience that gets to see this content. These are standard ads which you will often find on the right-hand side of their profile. Marketers also have the option of creating page post ads, which are promoted organic page posts.

- **SPONSORED POSTS:**

  Sponsored posts, on the other hand, are content which brands end up paying for to turn into an ad. For example, if one of your Facebook posts turned out to resonate really well with your audience and receive a really high engagement rate, brands actually have the option of paying to turn this into a sponsored content so that it gets seen by a wider audience base.

- **CAROUSEL ADS:**

    This is a great addition to Facebook's ad system because it allows a brand to advertise about 3 to 5 images, video content, or a mix of both at a time. This means that marketers will be able to feature multiple variations of their product in a single ad post.

- **CANVAS ADS:**

    These ads are commonly full screen and mobile optimized, and they feature a combination of videos, images, links, and texts to create a more overall immersive experience for the audience. Because these ads are highly interactive, they have the most potential for higher engagement rates. Audiences can choose to either zoom in, zoom out, click, play, pause or even swipe through the ad without ever having to leave Facebook.

1.3 Campaigning, Ad Sets, The Ad

2

Coming up with a strategy to guide the creation of ads can take some time. That being said, understanding how your ad is performing is crucial. It is very important to familiarize yourself with the important metrics and get data for **click-through rates (CTR)** and **cost per conversion (CPC)**.

The section dedicated for Campaigns, Ads and Ad Sets is a way for you to analyze your ads. You can choose the tab for the specific grouping you want to analyze. You can also use the **Breakdown and Performance columns** for more details.

Opening the Performance column will display a couple more options. From here, you can access specific aspects of the campaign. You can simply click one of the options to view related metrics.

Columns: Performance ▼   Bre

✓ **Performance (Default)**

Delivery

Engagement

Video Engagement

App Engagement

Carousel Engagement

Performance and Clicks

Cross-Device

Messenger Engagement

Offline Conversions

KPI's   ✕

Customize Columns...

Set as Default

Reset Column Widths

https://www.socialmediaexaminer.com/wp-content/uploads/2017/07/performance-report-options.png

Breakdown column opens up to more data. It can offer you specifics. For instance, if you want to know the specific days when conversions occurred or the device used by people when they clicked on your ad, this is the section that will display the information.

The columns can be further customized to come up with unique reports which you can share with your team. You can use it to analyze the performance and success of key metrics. For instance, when you care about knowing whether or not your ads perform 5% or above on click-through rate, you can set the columns so it shows the higher metrics at the top. After customizing your report, you can save it and use it for future reference. You can click on Save Report, name the report and complete the action by clicking Save in the dialog box.

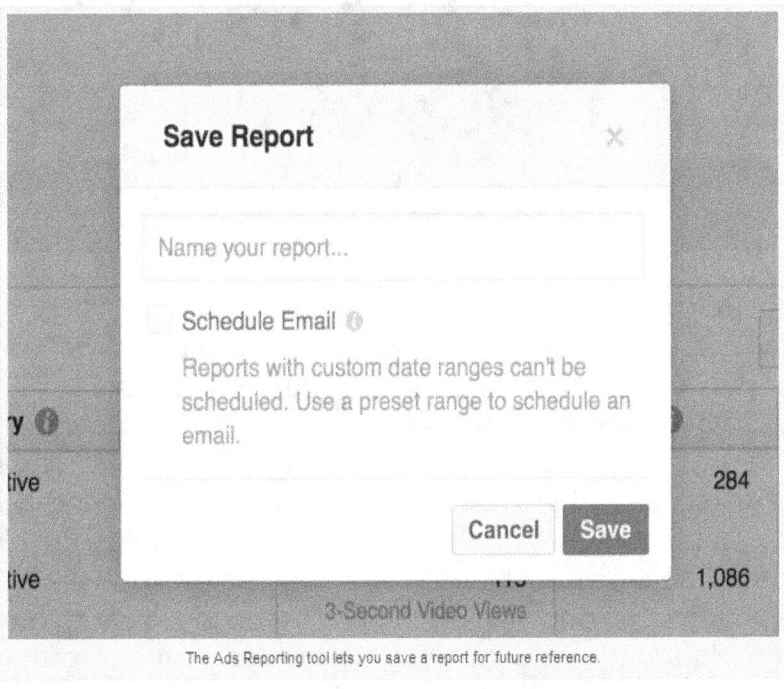

The Ads Reporting tool lets you save a report for future reference.

2.11.4 Facebook Business Manager

Security and control are among the things that business owners are concerned about. With Business Manager, you can easily manage your Facebook assets from your Pages to your ad accounts. It puts all these things together (in one place) and the best part is, it doesn't cost anything to set up!

Accessing the Facebook Ads Manager feature is easy enough. All you would have to do is head to the upper right-hand corner of any Facebook page, click on the drop-down arrow, and then select the **Manage Ads** option. You will then be directed to your Facebook ad account page, which you will be able to see a quick overview of your ad account. If you happen to manage more than one Facebook ad account, it is easy to tell go between both accounts too. All you would need to do is access the drop-down menu again and make the switch.

Depending on the size of your company, you may have more than one staff managing your social media profile. If that is the case, Facebook makes it easy for you to add your team members on to your Facebook ad account by granting them access. From there, you will even be able to assign them to their designated advertising roles. The roles could include that of an analyst, admin, or advertiser. This makes it easier for everyone involved to collectively manage your ad account as a team.

The Facebook Ads Manager dashboard is where you are going to do a lot of your management work. All the essential tools, buttons, and menus are going to be available on your dashboard for quick and easy access. There, you will find the option to create ads, find your filters, navigate you're spending over the last week, and even access a reporting table of all your Facebook ads.

Chapter 2: Create your Strategies

2.1 Develop your Strategies

The whole strategy is comprised of passion, people skills and communication skills. This is what separates the amateurs from the pros. Facebook is part of the strategy, not the whole strategy.

• YOU NEED PASSION

Why did you join your network marketing company? You can put every reason into two categories: you want to make more money or you want to have more time to do the things you love.

Want a new car, home or clothes for the family? That falls under "making more money." Want to see your children's basketball games or go on more family vacations rather than stay late at the office? These fall under "wanting more time in your life."

Understanding your passion keeps you going when times get tough. And they will. You are an entrepreneur now. You will also inspire everyone around you to chase their passion and never give up.

Think about it. Gini is ready to quit network marketing, so you give her a pep talk sharing your passion and why it means so much to have success in your network marketing company. She changes her mind and keeps pushing on. We understand because we've been there — several times!

• YOU NEED PEOPLE SKILLS

People need to genuinely like you and vice versa. You're helping people by showing the value of your product and business. If they don't feel a connection with you, they'll find someone else to work with — even if they love your company.

For example, let's say Mike is taking a look at your business. You're excited, smiling and focusing on him while talking about all of the fun the both of you will have if he joins. Do you think he might become a distributor? There's a good chance.

- ## YOU NEED COMMUNICATION SKILLS

You need to learn to get your point across with the least possible amount of words. Inspire others to become a customer and a distributor or refer you to someone else. You're excited. You believe you have the best product and opportunity in the world.

Once they're ready to join or buy, stop talking! If your friend is ready to be a customer, but you can't stop talking about every single feature, you may talk them out of taking action before you realize it.

- ## TALK WITH PEOPLE FACE TO FACE

Imagine one of your distributors, Amanda, just enrolled her fourth distributor in one month, and she lives 10 minutes from you. You congratulate her on Facebook so that everyone else can join in cheering her on. Now think about how much more excited Amanda will be when you invite her out to a celebration lunch, as well.

- ## TALK WITH PEOPLE OVER THE PHONE

As you build a team around the world, you can't meet with everyone face to face. The next best thing is a phone call. Did you know that your voice is as unique as your fingerprint? When we hear others' voices, we strengthen our relationships.

Steve, your newest distributor across the country, sends out 15 samples to friends and family in his first week. As always, you congratulate him on Facebook. Then you take that extra step and call him. He hears the excitement in your voice, and it motivates him to push beyond his comfort level. Steve hears, "You're doing a great job! I believe in you." No one ever believed in him before you. Do you think he's going to work even harder now? Yes.

- ## ATTEND COMPANY EVENTS

You might think you can stay online and never attend a company event, but you'd be mistaken. Those who attend company events develop a different type of appreciation for the product and opportunity. They're the most passionate distributors in the company because they hear the vision directly from the company owners and executive team. They spend quality time with other distributors from around the world who also attend. A culture is shared at events and attendees take that back to pass on to their teams.

Sherry is on the fence about becoming a distributor with your company. She decides to attend an event with you. She meets 10 more people who are as excited as you are, all sharing customer testimonials. Sherry gets excited and comes on board the next morning.

- ## PURSUE PERSONAL DEVELOPMENT

We all need to grow. We can all be better. We can't earn a six-figure income in network marketing without expanding our mind first. If you made $50,000 a year for the last 20 years, don't you think you need to change things about you in order to make $120,000? You do, and that change is between your ears. Most believe personal growth is the number one ingredient for success. We agree. Personal development happens by listening to audios, reading, attending events and having a personal coach.

- ## NETWORK MARKETING IS A NUMBERS GAME

It's easy to become frustrated when the people you know decide not to purchase your product or become a distributor. Rejection is the top reason people struggle with sales. You can ease your frustration by understanding the numbers of network marketing. On average, you will enroll one new distributor for every twenty people who look at your opportunity. For customers, it might be one out of every five who try a sample. Ask your company leadership to break down the numbers for your company. Understanding the numbers allows you to create a clear plan to success. Just because someone says no today doesn't mean they'll say no tomorrow. It's a timing issue. At some point in a friend's life, they might need your product or business. It's your job to stay in touch with them as a friend until the timing is right.

2.2 Advertising Strategies on Facebook

Consider using ActionSprout. If marketers think that Facebook pages are the real battlegrounds on Facebook, think again. Users typically interact with the page updates appearing in their news feeds apart from visiting the actual Facebook pages.

It is ideal for small scale business even though it is not recommended by some Facebook marketing experts. Do not hesitate to test this kind of technique.

After all, refusal of recommendation doesn't mean that this is ineffective and will not work.

Do split testing on Facebook ads. Finding the right keywords to use is crucial for Facebook advertising. To prevent wasting money, it is recommended to do a split advertising test first.

Allocate portions of advertising budget on running a variety of ads one at a time. Then, study the comparisons to assess which particular advertisement works best.

Only split testing can answer what particular benefit can a marketer get if he targets a narrow or wider audience.

Before anything else, it is important to plan ahead. This can give marketers enough time to develop Facebook marketing campaigns and incorporate these tips and tactics afterwards.

2.3 What is Facebook Marketing

Advertising on Facebook works along the same principles as regular advertising. If you want to achieve the return on investment from your advertising efforts, one of the keys to success is to ensure that you are focusing on the right group of people.

The more niche and narrower your target audience is, the better your return on investment will be. The logic behind this is simple, if your audience is far too broad and general, a lot of your efforts could be wasted on targeting those who are not even remotely interested in your content. To be effective with your marketing strategy, you need to aim for where it matters the most. This strategy will end up saving you a lot of time, money, and effort in the long run.

Another key to achieving success with your Facebook marketing is to ensure that your ad copy is just as well-targeted to your audience. A good approach to adopt in this instance would be to try and come up with a range of different ads. Each ad could target a particular challenge or problem that your current and potential customers have. This way, you will be able to draw in a much bigger audience base because of this wider marketing approach that you are taking. Instead of focusing on just one aspect or approach, you're now varying your range to aim for more people. Even within your niche audience, there are going to be different individuals with different needs. The more you're able to give them what they want, the more successful your marketing efforts will be.

Reasons to Start Advertising on Facebook Right Now

You'll be hard pressed to find any other social media platform which is going to allow you to meet your exact audience down to even the most detailed specifications the way Facebook can do for you. If you already know your audience well, you will be at an advantage because you could create highly targeted ads on this platform that make the huge impact.

If you are looking for a budget-friendly advertising platform that is still effective, look no further than Facebook advertising. How many other advertising channels out there will let you spend as little as $5 to reach 1000 people?

This is advertising at its fastest speed. From the minute you hit the click and submit button, your ad is going to be online for the whole world to see. Quite literally, the whole world. Audiences from all over the globe will be able to view your content in a matter of seconds if they're online. This gives your business the potential to reach thousands of people each day. This makes Facebook the fastest way for your business to drive conversions and traffic.

Because there is not one person out there today who is not familiar with Facebook, this makes it the perfect platform for you to start developing and building your brand awareness. Facebook is the go-to for anybody who is online, much like how Google is. The more familiar your audience becomes with your brand, especially when they see the strong presence that you have on social media, the more likely they will be to want to make a purchase from you.

Unlike Instagram, Twitter, Snapchat, or other social media platforms where words don't play a major role in promoting content, Facebook is different. This is where you get to be more descriptive with your captions, which will in turn help to drive traffic to your website.

There are plenty of ways in which Facebook makes a marketer's life significantly easier, one of this being that Facebook advertising is something which is easily measurable. There are no guessing games involved with this advertising platform. The results and the data will be there right in front of you, and the numbers will speak for themselves. With Facebook Insights and Analytics, you will be able to see in great detail the number of clicks you received, the conversions you got, and just how many impressions your post managed to garner.

Looking to increase your customer attribution? Then look no further than Facebook. Customer attribution is how many times your audience views your brand. The more often they see your brand appearing across their Facebook feed, the more likely they will be to convert to paying customers. That is because Facebook helps you increase the touch points with your audience, which eventually will lead to more conversions for your business.

Opting to advertise on Facebook will end up saving you a lot in terms of cost per acquisition moving forward. To advertise on this platform is so cost-effective and affordable that you will be able to save a lot of money not having to invest in other expensive advertising campaigns.

Remarketing is one feature that all brands love. Have you ever noticed how you randomly visit a website, and later when you log into your Facebook profile, you see the ad appearing on your newsfeed? It may seem like magic, but it's not. That's remarketing at work for you. Brands love this feature because it allows them to re-target audiences who have recently viewed or visited their website. If an audience visits the brand's website without taking any further action (like making a purchase for example), re-marketing gives that brand a second opportunity to re-engage with that audience through Facebook advertising. A simple tactic, but one that can dramatically boost conversion rates.

2.4 What are the Means of doing Facebook Marketing

Messenger

Facebook Messenger churns out around 1 billion messages every day. This includes those exchanged between friends and family, and those sent to business pages. As one of the most prominent messaging platforms currently available, almost everyone is available on Messenger. With such a wide base of users communicating through the app, being available on Facebook's ancillary communication channel makes it more convenient for consumers and prospects to reach out for you since they're probably already there.

When you activate Messenger for your Facebook account, you instantly enable a widget on your page that tells users how quickly you respond. According to statistics, users are more likely to message businesses on Facebook if it shows that they respond faster than others. In fact, Facebook even awards those that respond quickly to inquiries by giving their pages a badge the indicates a speedy response time.

The badge is shown just below the cover photo and helps improve messaging activity by telling prospective consumers that the page they are on will provide quick responses. While it might not seem like such an award to some, it's important to keep in mind that Facebook users **only spend an average of 41 minutes on the platform every day**. Knowing if a page responds quickly helps them push through with an inquiry since users typically prefer exchanges that don't take up too much of their limited Facebook usage time.

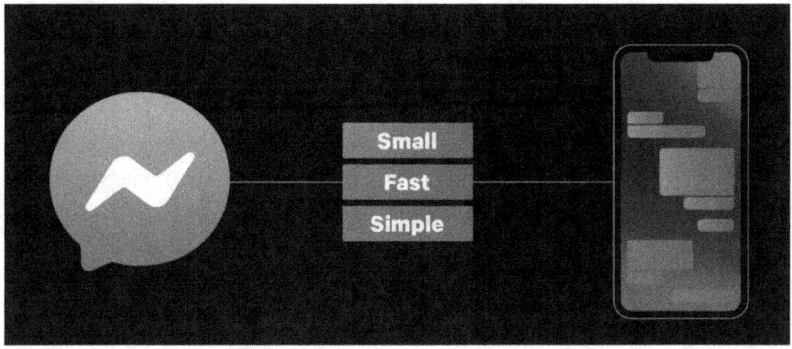

One of the Messenger features you can leverage for the purpose of reeling in more consumers is the automated response. Each time a user sends you a message, your Messenger will send an automated response that you set in order to provide primary, relevant information they might be looking for. Based on research, Facebook users that receive a response immediately after sending a message - whether or not it's automated - are more likely to hang around and wait for a business to send them more information to answer their inquiry.

Facebook lets businesses use a generic response upon activating the Response Assistant. To turn your page's automated response feature on, click the settings button along the upper right-hand side of your page's home screen and click the Messaging tab from the left-hand side panel.

Here you can access some of the essential settings of your Messenger application. The General settings basically help you control the standard features of your app, while the Response Assistant helps personalize your automated responses to get the best private engagement from your prospects and buyers.

The first feature of the Response Assistant is Instant Reply. Basically, this is what users will be greeted with if they send you a message on your page. Whether or not you're online, this message will be sent as an **immediate** response, since that's often what Facebook users look for. If you're online, this buys you some time to come up with an answer to their question or inquiry.

Facebook uses the response, "Thanks for messaging us. We try to be as responsive as possible. We'll try to get back to you soon," as their generic message for those who want to activate their Response Assistant. Marketers have the option to change it to their liking, and are also offered the opportunity to add personalization, such as the inquirer's name, a URL to the business's Facebook page, or the business's email address.

Experts recommend using something more fitting of your brand if you want to use the automated instant response. Something that resonates well with your company's identity will be seen as a much more authentic reply. Cold, automated, and detached generic responses - while better than no immediate response at all - are still generally received with some negativity.

Another Response Assistant feature you might want to look at is the reply it sends when you're away. You can set a specific schedule for the away message that your Messenger will provide inquirers so that it lets your market know that you're not there to attend to their needs, but that you will be once you go online. This feature sets expectations and helps make inquirers feel comfortable knowing their questions will be addressed soon. Again, setting the message to match your brand's identity is an important part of setting this feature.

Right before your prospects send a message, you could already provide them a welcome greeting that shows up prior to any conversation. This just sets the tone for your brand and helps Facebook users feel more comfortable and relaxed while communicating with you. Users who aren't 100% sure what they wanted to say might also be able to figure out how to talk to you to get their message across if they read your greeting.

Once you start an actual conversation with a Facebook user, you're essentially fulfilling the role of customer support. So, talk with respect and respond to each message objectively. Most Facebook users that have complaints will reach out to your page via Messenger to release some pent-up frustration and possibly offer correction where they find appropriate. As a brand, responding appropriately and humbly to these messages is an essential part of your marketing strategy.

Finally, it's important to respond **to every message** no matter how old it might be. This doesn't only improve your response rate, but also helps improve your reputation, helping Facebook users establish a more reliable and positive concept of your brand.

Comments

Comments are one of the most powerful tools you can use on your page. The more responsive you are to people's comments, the more likely they'll want to comment in the first place. That's because Facebook users often draw amusement from pages acknowledging their comments, especially if they were comical or simply social in nature.

This is yet another thing that the Walmart Facebook page seems to excel at, so everyone really could learn a thing or two from their strategy.

Here we see the page responding to a comment that wasn't an inquiry or a complaint. By simply responding to these comments - even if they're mundanely conversational - the brand effectively makes its audience feel more comfortable and familiar. This also helps drive more engagement since people are more likely to want to leave comments if they know they have higher chances of getting noticed.

As a page, you'll also find that Facebook users can get pretty nasty, especially if they've had a bad run-in with your brand. Poor product quality, lousy service, inefficient delivery schedules - these are all things Facebook users will loudly and proudly complain about through comments for all the world to see. So, the big question is - do you delete them?

The simple answer is **no. You shouldn't delete comments no matter how negatively they talk about your brand.** If you were to delete a comment even just seconds after it was posted, there's no guarantee that other Facebook users didn't see it as well. Because people tend to flock where there's drama, they will check back in and see that the comment had been removed. To Facebook users, this is often taken negatively, as if the brand were covering up for mistakes and complaints they don't want to confront.

Instead, use negative comments as an opportunity to improve your reputation. Showing instead that you care, that you're affected by the negative experience, and that you want to address the situation will prove that you mean **business.** This doesn't only prevent that one disgruntled buyer from spreading more negative reviews about your brand, but also helps assure others who might have saw the comment exchange that when they deal with you, they'd be in good hands.

Collecting Positive Reviews

Explore the internet in search of different marketing strategies and you'll find the reviews make up a large chunk of each and every one of them. The nature of the internet makes it convenient for anyone and everyone to gain access to **what others have to say.** And the fact that the venues for **sharing your thoughts and opinions** on the web are so vast and accessible, those who **have** something to say can easily find the right stage for it.

There are four reasons why people typically go out to post what they think about the products and services they receive. These include:

Significantly positive outcomes from the use of a product or the experience provided by a service. (i.e. impressive value for money, unexpected freebies, high-quality product performance or service provision, quick replies, and hassle-free transactions)

Significantly negative outcomes from the use of a product or the experience provided by a service. (i.e. too expensive for the quality provided, different from what's advertised, long waiting periods for both shipping and communication, unresponsive sellers)

Incentives for review submission such as loyalty points, exclusive discounts, or simply the opportunity to be featured on the page.

Partnerships with influencers that entail prominent social media users to write sponsored reviews to increase brand awareness amongst their followers.

Reviews are powerful selling points for your brand because they prove to others that you're reliable, legitimate, and that your products and services are truly worth the purchase. Of course, positive reviews don't generate themselves - you **need** to impress your buyers with real quality and value for money to deserve genuinely positive reviews.

To give you a better understanding of the importance and power of positive reviews (and reviews in general), consider these statistics:

87% of users rely on reviews to determine the reliability of a brand and its products

63% of Facebook page visitors specifically seek out negative reviews to validate any possible doubts they might have about certain products and services

Reviews without text that clarifies the reason behind the provided star rating are generally seen as fake and unreliable

40% of buyers will refuse to purchase from a brand if it has significantly detailed negative reviews on their page

60% of users will refuse to buy from a brand if it doesn't have any reviews at all

Generally, overall page ratings between 4.0-4.7 is where consumer interest peaks. Anything lower is considered unappealing, and anything higher is considered fake

While it's always ideal to have your buyers rate your brand and your items or services on their own volition, there are ways that you can encourage previous customers to provide reviews after they've received their products or services. For instance, on the Amazon marketplace, there are what they call Top Contributors that are given a designated badge each time they publish a review. This improves the trust that readers place on their opinions and ratings.

On Facebook, you can apply this by giving those who provide reviews the opportunity to be featured on your page. The simple possibility of receiving some attention on the social media platform helps make review writing more appealing.

What's more, you can also exchange loyalty points for Facebook reviews. For instance, one beauty brand encourages its buyers to write reviews for each verified purchase they avail through their website. Given that the items are purchased from the brand, reviews written will amount to one loyalty point each. Once the user reaches 30 points, they can receive an exclusive voucher that entitles them to $10 USD off on their next purchase.

The beauty of the scheme is three-fold:

It thickens their collection of reviews, making them a reliable source for user-generated opinions and feedback on a variety of beauty products

It encourages buyers to write reviews given the potential reward

It promotes loyalty. If a buyer has previously purchased and reviewed items from the brand, they'd feel more compelled to keep buying so they have more verified purchases to review, bringing them closer to the incentive

Of course, if you're just a humble start-up, you might not have a lot to offer in terms of incentives and rewards. So, you'll be happy to learn that there are things you can do to encourage positive review generation without having to shell out. Simply **asking** your buyers to write something about their recent purchase towards the goal of helping others to learn more about the products and services you offer can be highly effective. In fact, statistics have found that up to 80% of customers will write reviews when prompted - with or without the promise of any sort of reward or incentive.

That said, you do need to take into account the fact that this form of requesting reviews produces less passionately positive reviews. Since these users aren't really in it for anything, they're not likely to spend too much time talking about your products and services, especially if they weren't excessively impressed or disappointed. More often than not, they'll leave just a star rating. In some cases, they might write a line or two to give readers a rough idea of their experience. Will it be the most convincing user review your business will ever receive? Hardly. But it will generate more interest in your brand nonetheless.

Consumer Generated Content

Good reviews published by **real** consumers are easily trusted by audiences.
Why?
The fact that they were written from the perspective of someone regular people can relate to makes them a lot easier to believe. Plus, these regular folks aren't compensated for saying good things about the products or services they patronize, and so their reviews are likely just fueled by a strong desire to express gratitude and appreciation for genuinely satisfying goods and service provision.
While the best way to generate these real, raw, honest reviews would be to do your best with the services and products you provide, there are some techniques you can use in order to **encourage** your consumers to write them.
Dedicated brand hashtags give you an identity on the internet and encourage your buyers to **post** about your brand and your items. After all, how else would they use a

hashtag? Posting your hashtag online on your page, keeping a sign in your storefront that encourages people to use your hashtag, and adding your hashtag to photo posts helps it gain prominence. If you bring enough attention to it, it could become a mechanical necessity for your most avid shoppers.

One of the best viral brand hashtags we've seen so far comes from Coke with their #ShareACoke campaign. The personal touch encouraged buyers to post online, especially since the hashtag was debuted along with the personalized Coke packaging that features virtually every name conceivable.

Using hashtags along with the promise of momentary internet stardom is yet another way to generate original consumer-published content. Asking buyers to post about your products with your dedicated hashtag with the possibility of being featured on your page can be almost irresistible for some Facebook users.

Why?

While it might seem like being featured on a business page doesn't seem like too much of an accomplishment for most us, simply being given that attention and that exposure can easily satisfy any millennial. Internet culture has bred an inherent desire for likes, turning them into online currency. If you feature a Facebook user to your audience, they're likely to get more likes, which psychologically translates to popularity and approval - which everyone wants. Consider how Veet India did it.

The post doesn't go beyond offering users a chance to get featured, but it works. Remember - everyone's looking for a reason to post pictures on social media these days. It's all a part of the internet culture that these different platforms have stirred up in the human psyche. By giving them even just a trivial reason to share on their profile, they're much more likely to do so.

The addition of the hashtag makes it even more effective, allowing Facebook users to inform their friends that the post was published for a minor contest, encouraging more engagement. For you, the hashtag works because it makes it easier to sift through entries to find one that you can feature on your page.

You'd be surprised to find that a lot of the people who use social media actually have really intact concepts of photo composition and style. Smartphones have made it exceptionally easy to capture beautiful images. Some of them can be so good, in fact, that they can pass off as professional takes.

If you're lucky, there might be a few entries from Facebook users who have an exceptional eye for style and aesthetic. What you get out of the entire process is essentially **free advertising** - beautiful, powerful, user-generated content that you can post on your page to improve engagement and make your brand look even more trustworthy to your audience.

Another facet of user-generated content which we talked about a few chapters back is the process of enlisting the help of an influencer. These Facebook users are typically called **bloggers -** individuals who share regularly about their experiences to their wide online follower base through the use of social media. They're popular usually because they combine visually pleasing images with interesting or informational content. Travel, food, fashion, and other common interests people have are some of the niches these bloggers dwell in.

Considered a population between laypeople and celebrities, bloggers are the perfect middle-ground that makes them **more** relatable to their fan base compared to Hollywood stars because they're essentially just like everyone else - except for the fact that they have a keen eye for aesthetic and they have the means to do and experience things that many of us might consider luxuries.

To give you a better idea of what influencers can do for your brand, consider how Fashionova did it.

The business has built an entire enterprise by enlisting the help of some of the most prominent social media bloggers in the country and elsewhere. Without the use of **any** actual celebrities, Fashionova has managed to create an air of desire for their products by simply advertising their items through popular bloggers.

What's great about influencer marketing is that it **won't** cost you a lot. In fact, it might not cost you anything at all. For the most part, influencers will accept an invitation to advertise for a brand if:

They identify with your brand. Fashionova works with bloggers who dabble in the fashion, style, and makeup niches because their follower bases make up the audience that the brand wants to attract. If a blogger doesn't necessarily identify with your niche, or if they feel like your items don't match their preference, they're likely to decline the offer to team up. For you, choosing the right bloggers that resonate with your brand will help **sell** your products to your target market. Choosing an influencer that doesn't match your image could rub your audience off as unauthentic.

They get free items. Teaming up with an influencer doesn't really cost a lot. Simply sending over some of your items as freebies can make the deal difficult to decline. In exchange of the goods, you get a few social media posts, and a recommendation. Why should that be enough? Influencers typically have a very large, organic reach that they achieve with nothing more than quality content. This means that the people that follow them do so because they're genuinely interested in what these bloggers have to share and say. With that, it's safe to assume that whatever a blogger recommends will be greeted with a positive reception.

If you're wondering how to choose an influencer for your business, consider checking out relevant hashtags that relate to your business and your niche. The most prominent posts will likely come from the users with the highest follower count and the most engagement. Depending on the size of your brand, you may want to consider aiming for influencers that have a specific follower base.

For instance, influencers with millions of followers might only be interested in doing business with brands of significant size. That's not to say however that the case remains the same across the board. There are a few bloggers out there who would gladly team up, even with the smallest start-ups, but the likelihood of having them accept the offer might in some cases be a shot at the moon. In some cases, influencers might be bound by contracts with other businesses to prevent any conflict of interest. For instance, one influencer who already has a collaboration with one skincare brand might be restricted from engaging in a contract with another one. This simply eliminates the chance of confusing their follower base, especially because it creates competition between the two brands if they're both recommended by the same internet personality.

Another way to reach out to influencers is by seeking them out on platforms they might be more active on. These days, Instagram is the social media site of choice for bloggers who want to share their content. More often than not, though, these individuals also have Facebook pages that connect to their Instagram profiles. Which brings to light the next important aspect of Facebook marketing.

Chapter 3: Creating your Business Page

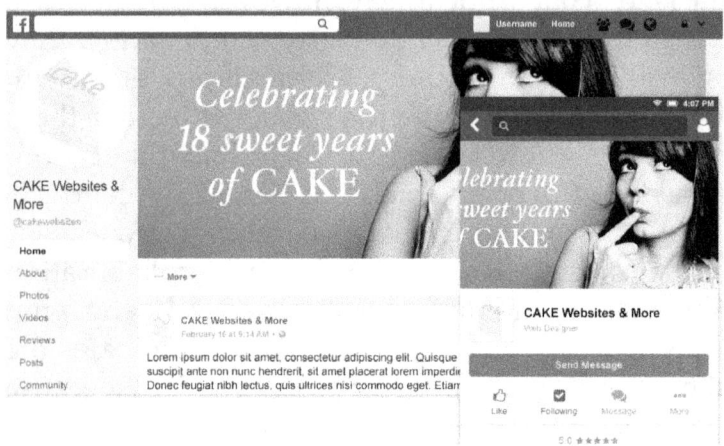

3.1 Account and Homepage: Defining your Brand

This Page will be attached to your Facebook personal profile. It is a separate entity, it works with an independent presence and can be used effectively to promote your brand, business or any cause. There are many features available to a Page that are not accessible to personal profiles. Among them are post scheduling, advertising and analytics.

3.2 Keyword Selection

Use descriptive keywords in the "About" section

The About section on your Facebook page is considered the primary source of textual property you own. Make sure the description of your business and products is as accurate as possible and use keywords that users can use when searching for their questions. While selecting the keywords, ensure that you go through other Facebook pages similar to yours and pick some keywords from there. Ask yourself, if someone had to search for your business or brand online, what are the words they would likely associate with your brand? Make a list of such words and keep it handy.

You should also always include the URL of your website in the description you provide. This will encourage users to click on it.

3.3 Optimizing your Page

Your Facebook page is the starting point for all your Facebook marketing efforts. It would be ideal if it were evaluated on both Google and Facebook so your customers and potential customers can easily find your brand. Once they have found your page, people should like the page. Here are some things you can do to optimize your site for the purposes mentioned above:

Choose a username that is meaningful and memorable

This type of URL is called a vanity URL. The web address of your Facebook page is your username for your Facebook page (e.g., www.facebook.com/name of your company). Each page is assigned a default URL consisting of numbers. Your username should be such that it reflects the topic of your page or the name of your entire company so that search engines and customers can easily find your business in Google and Facebook searches. You need at least 25 likes if you want this URL.

Optimize the images on your page

The first thing people see when they visit your site is your cover image and profile photo. The images you use should be of good quality and reflect what your brand wants to emit. The images used must be of reasonable size. This means that the photo on the cover should be about 851 x 315 pixels in size, and the profile image should have a size of 160 x 1160 pixels. Avoid grainy or poor-quality images. The images you use must also be relevant to your brand or business and should not be random. For example, if you are a local restaurateur, then posting images about the latest developments in the automobile industry doesn't make any sense.

Pinned posts

No matter what you think, most users only visit your page once. They are interacting with your page through the news displayed in their newsfeed, but they don't usually open your business page over and over again.

For this reason, the main function of your page is to convince the user to click the Like button. Facebook allows the page administrator to attach a message to the top of the page. Make sure that the topic of this post, which can be attached, is interesting and unique and attracts the attention of the page visitor.

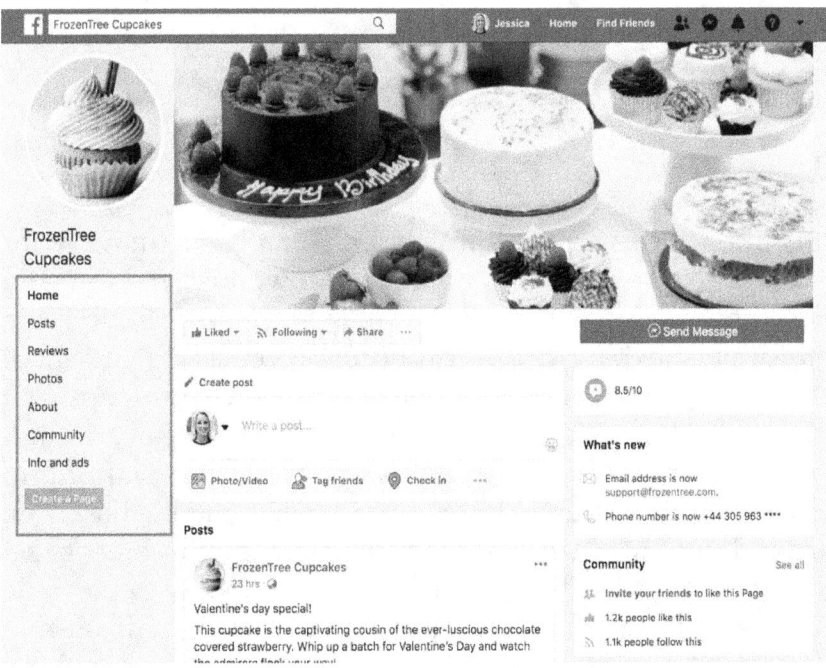

3.4 Post, Content, Images, Video, Posting link

Images

It is likely that you have uploaded some basic imagery for your page upon creating your site. Now, it is time to really nail down your "look" and master it. When you are building or expanding your online presence, it is essential that you get it properly. Having a poor quality image that does not look visually appealing and can greatly inhibit your success because it prevents people from wanting to look at your content. Remember, social media has been around for a while now which has allowed marketers to set the bar pretty high. While it certainly runs by achievable high standards, you do have to do more than simply throwing up a basic image and calling it a day. Everything needs to look a specific way to attract your audience and encourage them to follow and engage with your site.

Here is what you need to do to create a custom image that attracts your target audience.

Find Your Edge

Before you really dig into creating your image, it is a good idea to find your edge. This requires you to take a look at your competition and see what they are doing on Facebook. Take some time to identify what their theme is, what color scheme they are using, and how it is helping them interact with your shared audience. You may begin to notice a trend of what color schemes and themes seem to work best with your audience. When you do notice this trend, use it to help you identify your own way of fitting into the marketplace.

The key to finding your edge is knowing what everyone else is doing and then doing it better. You want to see what is helping others succeed and then customize your own theme and color scheme that looks and performs better than anyone else's. When you do this, you begin to create a unique look that supports you in having a greater impact on reaching your target audience. When they see why you are different and better, they are more interested in following you.

Get A Logo and Cover Art Made

Facebook allows you to have a profile picture and cover art. While you can easily throw up any image, having branded images looks infinitely better. You can make this yourself, but it is recommended that you leave it to a graphic designer. Having an image that is attractive and that accurately represents your business is important. Facebook's sizing differences between mobile and desktop can sometimes make images blurry, so having a professional create your images can save you a headache and give you the opportunity to have great imagery that looks high quality as well. Remember, blurry, pixelated, or otherwise low-quality photographs will not suffice in online marketing in the 21st century.

Great places to hire professional graphic designers for a reasonable fee include Upwork, Fiverr, and 99 designs. Websites like Upwork and Fiverr will typically only charge around $5-$10 per image which makes them incredibly affordable. 99 designs do cost quite a bit more, but they also give you many options to choose from and tend to have higher quality imagery. You should choose the one that best fits your budget and needs.

Creating an Attractive Profile

Creating an attractive profile requires two things: static content that is consistent and high quality, and posts that are consistent and high quality. You want to maintain the same color palette and theme throughout your whole page. While not every single picture you post may be rooted in your color scheme, it should make sense to your overall theme and look attractive on the page that you are creating.

Pay attention to how you are posting, what you are posting, and how it all fits with what you are sharing overall. If anything does not make sense or does not amplify or enhance the overall aesthetic, theme, and message of your page, then you should refrain from posting it. Staying higher quality and trendy is important because it ensures that people enjoy scrolling your page and are more likely to follow you and revisit your page on a regular basis.

Where to Find Images for Posting

Finding images to post on your page can sometimes be challenging. However, it does not have to be. There are a few things that you need to know, however. The first thing is that you should be seeking images that are free of copyright. Royalty-free stock images are a great place to start because they provide you with great, high-quality images that you do not have to credit anyone for when you are using them. Plus, you do not have to worry about copyright infringement! Websites like Pixabay or Unsplash are great ones to go to for searching what images you want to use on your page. You can easily save the images and share them on your page with whatever caption and content you desire. Additionally, you can easily search for images that suit your theme and color scheme, so that they stay on-brand and keep your page looking beautiful and attractive to your audience.

Videos

Facebook understands that people want different kinds of videos in different situations. For instance, if someone is on their mobile device, they are probably on-the-go and would prefer to watch something short. Meanwhile, if a person is on a larger device (like a laptop) and sitting on the couch, then they are likely more willing to watching a longer video.

For shorter videos, you might want to consider using in-feed ads. Whether your goal is to reinforce your brand or promote a new product, in-feed ads capitalize on quick, short spurts of attention from your target audience to promote your business.

Create a captivating video which quickly tells your story, and people, while scrolling through their feed, will stop to hear what your company has to say. Using video ads is a great way to drive sales. Furthermore, by combining video ads with product images and carousels, you can stimulate the interest of your audience and potentially increase your sales.

You can also create video ads that appear "in-stream," meaning the ad is shown after the viewer has begun watching a video. In-stream video ads can be as long as fifteen seconds, but the shorter they are, the better. Research shows that 70% of in-stream ads are watched to completion, with the audio/ sound on. This allows you to deliver a more dynamic message to your audience.

Another advantage to using video ads on Facebook is that it allows your company to reach people that you might not otherwise reach with more expensive television ads. Research shows that Facebook video ads reach 37% percent more people in the age group of 18 to 24. Facebook is also creating new ways of using video to engage your audience. With Facebook 360 your much more eye-catching and attention-getting than a simple picture!

Finally, using Facebook Creative Hub, you can create "mock-up" or tester video ads, and then test them in real time. This allows you to see how various types of video ads may affect your audience and allows you to view these video ads from the perspective of your audience. This is especially important if you are interested in running a video ad in the News Feed of mobile phones, as the Mobile-view can restrict what appears on the screen.

As always, make sure the images you are using are either free of copyright or that you own the copyright or copyright release to them.

3.5 Optimizing posting time

The reason why so many people love Facebook is that it is simple and easy to use. Even creating ads on this platform couldn't get any easier. To create your first ad, all you need to do is head to the Facebook Ads Manager where you will find a prominent green button on the upper right-hand corner which says **Create Ad**.

Once you have clicked on the button, you will be presented with a choice of about 15 different objectives which would they need to choose from. The objective could include promoting your Facebook page, boosting posts, and even getting more audiences to install your app. It would depend on what your goal is for creating this ad.

Even after you have successfully created your ad if at any point you feel that you need to edit it, no problem. To edit your existing at, all you need to do is hover over the name of the ad, and then click on the edit icon. There will be a pop-up which will slide in on the right side, and this will enable you to quickly edit any changes you need to make to your ad. The great thing about Facebook Ads Manager is that it allows you to edit multiple ad campaigns or even at sets at once. This definitely saves a lot of time and effort on your part too.

For ad campaigns, the changes that you will be able to make with Facebook Ads Manager include being able to edit the name of the campaign, switching your campaign either on or off, and even setting a campaign spending limit which is optional. For regular Facebook ads, what you would be able to edit with the name of the ad, the creators of the ad, whether it is switched on or off, and the destination of your ad.

For Facebook ad sets, what you would be able to edit would be the name of the ad set, the ad placement, the target audience, the budget, and the schedule, whether the asset is on or off, and even the optimization and delivery of your ad set.

Chapter 4: Creating Audience list for Facebook Ads

4.1 How to create an Audience List

What some beginners think is that establishing an identity comes **before** discovering an audience. In most cases however, it's the opposite. Before you start posting and decide what you want, it's important to first pinpoint **what your audience** wants to see. Different products and services from different niches cater to unique consumer **personas** - an abstract collection of concepts and characteristics that businesses attribute to their target market in order to meet their standards and preferences.

On Facebook, there are more than a handful of different **personas** that you might find, so narrowing your business's target to just one or two can help make your efforts more fruitful.

Consider this: Two businesses, **Business 1 and Business 2** have both just opened their Facebook Pages to extend their reach and become available to their market on the biggest online platform currently available.

BUSINESS 1

is a furniture retail store that offers low-priced pieces that are mainly made from composite material. They're light, budget-friendly, and they come in large quantities since they're mass-produced in the company's factories. While some products are available for purchase through their partner furniture stores in some malls, most of their items can be found through their website, which is the main focal point of their revenues.

BUSINESS 2

is a bespoke furniture manufacturer. They sell high-end solid wood pieces made from maple, New Zealand pine, and birch wood. Their pieces are heavy, one-of-a-kind, and unique, with only one stock available per design. They have a studio where their items can be found and purchased, which is the main center of their business. Facebook and all other online channels are simply for the purpose of information dissemination - they share info on how to take care of solid wood, how to tell apart different kinds of wood, and other interesting articles that are published on their official blog.

Both brands sell furniture, that's true. So, you might say they're in the same niche. But do you think there's competition between these two? And more importantly, do you think they should be appealing to their markets with the same strategies?

While both Business 1 and 2 operate in the furniture market, they've got two completely different goals. The first aims to provide its buyers with budget-friendly options that are easily accessible over the internet and through several retail stores in key malls in their locality. The second leans more towards **art**, selling furniture not for its inherent usefulness, but for its beauty. So, the brand caters mostly to collectors and high-income individuals who have the luxury of paying for investment-like items.

All things considered, it goes without saying that Business 1 and Business 2 are trying to appeal to completely different consumer personas. Here's a quick draft of what those personas might be:

Business 1	**Business 2**
Budget-conscious buyers	Willing to spend more
More interested in function rather than form	In search of unique pieces that are more aesthetically appealing than functional
Looking for a quick purchase	Willing to take their time, as well as travel to the actual store to make a purchase
Not necessarily interested in an investment	Looking for a furniture investment with resale value

Now that this idea has been established, both brands can now come up with an aesthetic and identity that they can fly with to make sure they're appealing to their audience in the best way possible.

In the same light, it's important that you consider the specific needs, preferences and thoughts of your buyers. In doing this, you won't waste your time or effort coming up with marketing material that will fly over their heads.

To establish an idea of your Facebook consumers' persona, ask yourself these questions:

WHAT AGE ARE THEY?

- Looking back at the example shared above, it's easy to assume that the first business would probably appeal more to younger buyers - college students, small families, single professionals - those who might be more interested in the function of the item rather than the way it looks. The second business would be better off aiming their marketing strategy at older individuals with the money to spend on such expensive pieces, and those who could see the inherent value of solid wood.

Knowing the age of your consumer persona can make it possible for you to communicate with them in terms that they understand. Typically, younger generations respond better to brands when they adopt the current language, including meme culture and slang. For older individuals, sophisticated, professional tones of voice tend to communicate ideas more effectively.

WHAT'S THE NATURE OF THEIR WORK?

- You might think that your audience's employment shouldn't matter, but the significance of their work lies in the fact that it tells you more about their schedules. Facebook users who are office workers might be offline from 9 to 5, and online for the rest of the day as they commute home or relax in their own space. Retirees can be online any time of the day, so your peak hours for activity can be anywhere from the early hours of the morning until late in the evening, with a few dead spots in the middle as our seniors take their naps.

Consider the kind of products and services you're offering and try to figure out the specific work demographic that might be interested in them. For the most part, this technical part of discovering your target market might be a topic all on its own. However, there are tools you can find online and use to help you learn more about the possible employment categories that might be most interested in what you offer.

HOW MUCH DO THEY MAKE?

- A large part of knowing how much your target makes relies on knowing where they work. Understanding your buyer's budget is an essential aspect of marketing anywhere on the internet. On Facebook however where almost everything is visual, knowing how much your buyers are willing to spend will help you format your pictures and other media to communicate the cost of your services and products.

For instance, recent surveys have found that brands that tend to leverage fun, colorful images with lots of quirky graphics and playful fonts are typically characterized as budget-friendly. Those that use dark images with less colors, dramatic imagery, and a sleek, sophisticated overall appeal are branded expensive and high-cost.

Why should this be important? Knowing how much your target audience can spare for services or products like those you offer can help you format your posts to meet their expectations at a glance. Tailoring your posts to communicate that your products and services meet their financial freedom to spend will make it more likely for them to click through and learn more about you.

If, for example, a person who doesn't know your brand sees your post on their feed and finds that you sell something they could possibly want or need, then you might spark an interest.

But once the initial discovery moves to the next phase of the consumer flowchart - which is determining cost - they might shy away from your brand if it doesn't meet the price they're willing to pay. If you look too expensive, your budget-minded audience might feel you're out of reach. If you look too affordable, those who have the luxury to spend might question the quality of your offers.

If you fail to communicate the right cost range with the way you market yourself on your Facebook, you could lose those valuable clicks that bring potential consumers to your page in the first place.

4.2 Understanding the Marketing Objective

If you are already a regular user of Facebook, you would be familiar with seeing ads pop up on your sidebar or in between your newsfeed every now and then. That is Facebook advertising at work. The ads will appear on the audiences' page through either paid search or another option called paid social. In paid search, what happens is this option helps the audience find and locate a company. Paid social, on the other hand, helps the company find the audience.

A business can actually target its audience using Facebook's user data which is accumulated based on the audiences' likes, views, Facebook activity, and what they have shown an interest in. Now, you are probably wondering why Facebook advertising could prove to be the best bet for your business. Why should you invest your precious time and resources into marketing your brand on this social media site compared to others?

Facebook advertising is a good option for your business because it is still among the cheapest ways for you to advertise online. It even outperforms other traditional web ads and Google ads. Not only is it the more affordable option but also allows you to target your audience effectively, aiming to get your message out there in the most precise manner to the audience that matters the most. This makes it one of the most effective methods of online marketing and advertising. With more than 2 billion people actively using this platform, those numbers speak for themselves in terms of potential. Target your audience in the right way, and you stand to boost your business sales and brand awareness like never before.

Leveraging on the potential of Facebook advertising will also enable your business to reach global audiences in a matter of seconds. Facebook is a worldwide phenomenon, and there is no better platform out there to help your brand boost its digital media exposure and double, maybe even triple sales, just by expanding your reach.

4.3 How to increase Visibility on your Post

A common complaint that the majority of site owners share is that most of their fans have not seen their posts on Facebook. Facebook successfully studied this problem, and they managed to narrow the problem down to two main factors.

The first is the amount of content published on Facebook. This means that the user's newsfeed does not have enough space to display each message. The competition for publishing and appearing in the user's newsfeed is very stiff, and this results in a reduction of the impact on regular posts.

The second reason for limiting the visibility of the post is that the Facebook algorithm has been designed to display only the content most relevant to its users. Relevance is now determined by many factors, including the way a person interacted with a page in the past, the type of posts published, and the popularity of previous posts on the page among its users. Simply put, the more popular your posts are, the more visible they are. The following two tips can improve the visibility of your posts in the fan feed.

Using video in your publishing strategy. Videos are more attractive and can help attract the viewer's attention.

Look at the Insights page to determine the type of content that appeals to your audience. Page Insights typically contain a lot of content-type data that can help you interact more with your audience. Find out about the formats of the messages that are most visible (images, videos, links, or lyrics) and topics that appeal to your audience. Also, keep track of the days and times, as well as the frequency of publishing, that seem to work very well with your audience.

To get the most out of your advertising, you need to make sure the content you provide is attractive. Yes, you can use Facebook to publicize your business, but this is also an opportunity to create and maintain lasting relationships with your target audience. Ask yourself, "Will my fans find this article interesting for reading and interacting, even if they are not interested in buying a product I offer?"

Chapter 5: Install Facebook Pixel

It is highly recommend that you set up your Facebook Pixel as it is the best way to enjoy Facebook Business Manager. It is simply a set of codes that Facebook helps you to generate so when you place it on your website or on Facebook with the help of cookies, it grants you access to information to help you optimize your ads, track conversations, remarket leads, and build target audiences for ads.

Facebook Pixels are of so much importance that we advise that you set it up right away, even if you are not ready to start your ad campaign yet. This is because it helps to start collecting data as soon as it is installed so by the time you are ready to start creating your ads, you will already have enough ads to work with.

The main thing these pixels do for you is that they help you get the best out of your ad campaign. They make sure that your ads reach the desired people who are most likely to take action. With this, your investments do not go to waste as you are sure of higher conversion rates.

Below are some of the ways Facebook Pixels can help you increase the results of Facebook Marketing:

Helps in tracking your Facebook conversion rates: You do not have to launch your ads and leave its success to fate because you are in the dark about how the ads are performing. With Facebook Pixels, you can track the performance of your ads by knowing about the interaction of your audience with your website after they have viewed the ads. This simply means that you will be able to track the conversion rates of your ads.

Not only can you track the activities of the ads, but you can also track the activities of customers across devices. This means that you will know whether people switch to desktop after viewing your ad on mobile or maybe if it's the other way around. This information will help you to re-evaluate your ad campaign strategy to know whether or not you need to refine it. Also, it will be easier for you to calculate your return on investment.

Facebook Retargeting: There are some customers that have already interacted with your site through your ads but haven't taken any marketing action. These are the one that your retargeting ads are for. With the help of Facebook retargeting data and dynamic ads, you will be able to reach customers who have shown interest in certain products on your site. For example, if someone already visited your website and added a product to their wish list or cart, your retargeting ads will have to be that of the product they are interested in. This is a way of reminding your potential customers that their preferred products are waiting for them so they can come for it when they are ready.

Creates lookalike audiences: Facebook can help you expand your audience by helping you to reach people who have the same likes, interests, and demographics with those that are already interacting with your website. Through this, you will get more people to know your brand and some of these people will certainly convert into real customers.

Optimize your ads to increase conversions: You can use the data provided by Facebook tracking pixel to boost your ads for particular conversion events on your website. Without a tracking pixel, you will only be able to optimize conversions like click links. Pixels, however, help you to optimize those conversions that align closely with the goals of your business.

Optimize your ads for value: This is made possible by the data Facebook collects on those that buy from your website through Facebook and how much they have spent on the site. This data can help you optimize your ads' audience based on their value. What this means is that Facebook will show your ads to those customers that are likely to make big purchases.

Grants you access to more Facebook tools and Metrics: The only way you can get to use some Facebook tools is by installing Facebook Pixels. For example, if you want to use custom audiences for your website, web conversion campaigns, or dynamic ads, you will need Facebook Pixel. In addition to this, Pixels helps you to know the cost of your campaign by tracking metrics like cost per conversion or cost per leads.

A Guide on Using Facebook Pixels

Now that you already know the great benefits that Facebook Pixels has, it is time to learn how to put this tool to great use.

Here are ways you can use Facebook pixels to gather data on two different kinds of events (specific actions that your website's visitors take on the site), these are:

Facebook standard events, which are the platform's predefined set of 17 standard events.

Customized events which you have set up yourself.

Facebook Pixel's 17 Standard Events

Below are 17 predetermined Facebook pixel events whose codes you can simply copy and paste:

- **Purchase:** Someone who has successfully made a purchase on your site.

- **Lead**: A person who has signed up for a trial or on the other hand, identified themselves as a leader on your page.

- **Complete Registration**: For a person that has successfully completed a registration form like a subscription form on your site.

- **Add Payment Information**: When someone adds their payment information on the website, in the process of making a purchase.

- **Add to Cart:** When a person adds your product to their shopping cart on your website.

- **Add to Wishlist**: A person includes a product to their wishlist on your website.
- **Initiate Checkout**: Anyone who begins the process of checking out to buy something on your website.

- **Search**: Anybody who makes use of the search function on your website to look for a particular product on the site.

- **View Content**: When a person lands on a specific page on your website.

- **Contact**: Someone who reaches out to your business.

- **Customize Product**: Someone selects a specific variant of a preferred product.

- **Donate**: When a person gives freely to your cause..

- **Find Location**: When someone initiates a search for the physical location of your business.

- **Schedul**e: Anyone who books an appointment with your business.

- **Start Trial**: A person who signs up for a free trial period of your product.

- **Submit Application**: A person applies for any of your products, services, or events.

- **Subscribe:** When a person completes a subscription for a paid product or service.

Also, you can add extra codes known as parameters to add details to standard events. This will help you to customize standard events based on currency, basket contents, content type/ID, and the worth of conversion event.

Facebook Pixel's Custom Events

Custom Events is a feature that helps you get more details than those provided by Facebook Pixel's standard events or to customize events to suit the peculiar needs of your website in place of standard events. These types of events make use of URL rules which depends on the rules of specific URLs or URL keywords.

To create custom events in place of standard events, go to the 'Custom Conversion Section', then click on 'Create Custom Conversion'. Add the URL or part of the URL already copied from your website, which represents your custom event. In a case where you are making use of URL Equals, ensure that you also add the domain e.g. 'www'. It is unnecessary for you to include 'HTTP' or 'https'.

If you are using a different analytics tool, take a look at the list of your page views there, then copy and paste the exact URL.

Once this is done, the next thing you should do is to select a category and click 'Next'.

You are expected to give a unique name to your custom event and provide a description of it. If applicable, you should also add a conversion value. Note, however, that our conversion values are expected to be in whole numbers, without additional characters like the dollar sign. Including conversion values helps you to keep track of your ROI. Once you have entered all necessary pieces of information, click 'Done'. You can now create your ad using the objective of your website conversion by selecting the custom event you want to optimize, then track that event.

Split Standard events with Custom Conversions

If you discover that you need more customization when you are already using standard events, you can help yourself out with custom conversions. For example, if you have a shoe line and you are already using the View Content standard events for your products but want to optimize for different categories, you can do this using custom events. When doing this, apply the same rules for URL create conversions for our different categories.

P.S.: In case the URL rules do not apply to your website, you can use events to create custom conversions and add parameters.

Creating Facebook Pixels to Add to your Website

Now that we are done learning what we can track on our website using Facebook Pixels and why we would want to track them, let us now consider creating these pixels and putting them to work on our websites.

To create Facebook pixels, click on Business Settings' on your Business Manager Dashboard, choose 'Pixels' on the 'People and Assets' tab on the left-hand side then click 'Add'.

You will now give a name to your pixel, by entering no less than 50 characters on the space provided, then click create. Before you create, make sure you go through Pixels' terms and conditions because you are agreeing to them once you use the service.

Wait for a moment for your pixel to be created then click on 'Set up the Pixel Now'.

The last step to take in creating your Facebook pixels is to follow the detailed instructions on your Facebook pixel guide carefully, to start collecting data by setting up pixels on your website.

Keep in mind that Facebook allows you to create ten pixels when you are using Facebook Business Manager.

Create your First Ad Campaign on Facebook Business Manager

Now that you have successfully set up your pixels, you can now create your first ad with confidence that it will do relatively well.

To create an ad, click on 'Business Manager' at the top left-hand side of your Business Manager Dashboard. There, you will see the 'Create and 'Manage' tab, click the ads manager then click on the green 'Create' button.

You will receive a pop-up, and there, select 'Guided Creation' then choose the objective of your campaign, target it to an audience, set budget and schedule, and choose your preferred type of ads according to the different types of ads.

There you have it! With these steps, you are now ready to make the most out of Facebook with everything you need in one spot, to get the greatest results out of your ads and other Facebook marketing efforts, thanks to Facebook Business Manager. Let us now take a critical look at Facebook advertising to know the best ways to tweak your ads, the best industry practices, as well as some dos and don'ts to get ample results from your ad campaigns.

Chapter 6: Facebook Retargeting

6.1 How to use Facebook Retargeting

Not everyone wants to participate in polls, and not everyone wants to click through a link you provide to read a full-length article. So, before you publish any content, think about your audience and what they'd like to see to encourage engagement.

For instance, a page targeting mothers and grandmothers with family-related content might leverage heartfelt quotes pasted over visually stimulating images to tap into their readers' emotions. This content generates shares, tags, and comments, as their audience might feel a sense of familiarity or because the content might encourage memories of days long gone to resurface.

This is in contrast to a travel page that offers its reader's domain links that redirect to their website where they share information on the latest travel destinations and hotspots the world over.

Why would their audience be willing to click through?

Simple - because a blog on a travel destination will likely provide a more accurate representation of the experience when compared to a Facebook post. They're not likely to find that kind of content on the social media platform anyway since it can get pretty long, so they'd be more than willing to read about it elsewhere.

Different formats work for different people with different interests - it's just the way social media works. Trying to put yourself in their shoes and listing what you prefer in the content you are interested in and what you typically find to be a nuisance can help establish the best format for your brand.

Presently, this information might not mean a lot to you and you might not concretely understand how to use it. But in the following chapters, discussions of how to use Facebook will make it easier to put this knowledge into motion.

For now, it's time to open up your new Facebook page to reach the billions of users waiting to meet your brand.

6.2 How to creating a retargeting Campaign on Facebook

Facebook ads are a type of ad referred to as PPC. If you have been marketing online for any length of time, then you should be familiar with this term. To recap, PPC means 'Pay Per Click', which in turn means that you only have to pay for the ad each time someone clicks on it.

You will set a maximum amount you are willing to pay for each click on each ad. So, for instance, if you set your maximum CPC (Cost Per Click) to be 50 cents, then that means you will get a minimum of 20 clicks a day before you spend more than your daily budget.

In truth though, you may get more clicks than this. That's because Facebook ads work on a bidding system. When there is a 'space' on the site for an ad to show to a specific customer, Facebook will then look to the ad campaigns it has live and find the relevant options.

A bidding war will then be carried out between those different ads, so that the one with the highest CPC will end up being shown.

That said, the advertiser will only pay the amount they need to in order to win the bid. So, if all the other ads in your niche only set their CPC to 20 cents, then you will only pay 21 cents per click, thus getting a lot more clicks in total!

So, if you set your CPC too low, then you will lose out on the bids and your ads won't show – or will only show a few times, to less competitive audiences.

That said though, if you set your CPC too high, then you'll only reach a few people before you exceed your budget and your ads stop being served for the day.

And so, there is a highly precarious balancing act that must take into account all three of these factors: the competitiveness of the niche, the CPC, the daily budget… and you thus must choose the right amount to spend.

Do you aim for a smaller niche with fewer people, and thus be able to get more exposure for a lower cost? Or do you compete head to head with the big players, and perhaps only get your ad displayed once or twice?

As ever, the best option is often to work your way up. When you're a small business with a small budget, aim for smaller sub-sections of the market and try to establish yourself there. From that point onward, you can then try to reinvest the profits you make in order to expand your reach further and further and compete with the bigger brands.

If you're brand new, then targeting males interested in fitness between 20-30 with a supplement brand will be out of your price bracket as you compete with big supplement companies, Amazon, and Bodybuilding.com.

But if you target martial artists who do Brazilian Jujitsu with the same product, all located in a specific area, then you might be able to make a dent.

The other thing to consider is your CLV – Customer Lifetime Value. In other words: how much do you stand to earn from each of these ads? And therefore, how much should you realistically be willing to spend on each ad?

The best-case scenario is that someone sees your ad, clicks on your ad, and then visits your site to buy your product. Remember: you only pay each time someone **clicks** on your advert. So as long as you earn more from each visitor than you pay for each click, your ads will **make** more money than they cost you. If you make $30 profit for each sale, then that should be very easy.

But of the 100 people who visit your website, it's likely that only one or two will **actually** buy a product. That's a 1-2% conversion rate, which is actually considered to be pretty good.

That means that the 'average' value of each visitor to your site, is closer to $30 / 100 – so 30 cents.

If you consider though that a few people might sign up to your mailing list and buy later, or might buy more than one product, then you can potentially increase the number to 60-70 cents. This is why it's called the **lifetime** value – it's the lifetime of the customer. You might take a while to see this return though, which is why you also need to consider your cash flow.

Either way, make sure you are earning money from your campaign on average, before you start spending.

Chapter 7: Creating a Facebook Ad Campaign: How to be successful

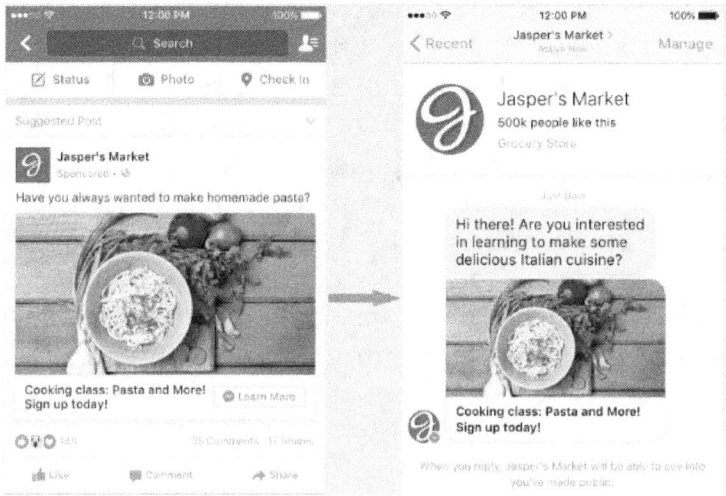

7.1 The sales conversion process

A tool like Facebook's Conversion Pixel comes in handy here to help you monitor just how many conversions your advertisements are returning, along with the cost of each one. This pixel is a code for your website, and with this code, you will be able to measure your ad's performance. It also enables you to optimize your audience building by ensuring your content gets delivered to the people who are most likely going to act on it. The Facebook pixel tools work by reporting each time someone pays a visit to your site and takes some form of action (like making a purchase, for example). This allows you to know precisely when an action has been taken as a result of your ad, and thanks to Facebook's Custom Audience feature, you can easily target the same audience again. The better your conversion rate gets, the better Facebook becomes in terms of delivering your ad content to those more likely to take action. This process is known as conversion optimism.

The perfect Facebook ads are attractive and get the point across immediately. It does not annoy people with boring details or sales pitches full of business jargon. When crafting your ad, the way to go is to make it conversational and relaxing. You can use headline analyzers to find out how good your headlines are. The best ones are those that are clear, concise, and conversational. It could be a straightforward benefit of a service or product or a list of things to do to achieve a certain something or even a clever phrase.

7.2 Promoting page posts

Some businesses or brands make conversions with their content. Take for example the Goodful Page from Buzzfeed, which makes commissions off of affiliate marketing content that makes conversions. They present the products through their viral video and provide a link for viewers to make a purchase if they find the products of interest. They also have their own line-up of household essentials that Facebook users can learn more about through their page.

So naturally, driving traffic to their Facebook page is a major necessity in their attempt to increase sales and improve the ROI of their brand. In this case, ads that promote page popularity becomes an integral part of the Facebook marketing strategy.

Much like the ads that promote your business locally, these ads can be targeted to users of a specific age, gender, and locality, and they can be set to show an image, a video, or multiple products that viewers can swipe through. The CTA button though can only be set to Like the business's page, and the locations for publications are limited to Facebook. These ads can show up on the Feed and along the side panel of the desktop Facebook website.

Promoting your Facebook page with ads like these can be incredibly beneficial if your brand communicates most of its messages through its page. For affiliate marketers and viral news pages, this type of ad often proves to be most effective.

7.3 Getting more links and click to your website

These ads are ideal for businesses and service providers that use their website more actively than their pages. For instance, Upwork - a freelancing platform that connects businesses with independent professionals - performs all of its functions through their website. This is where users log in, interact with clients and freelancers, and get paid. So, anyone who might want to use Upwork should access their website to get the most out of the platform's benefits and functions. That said, the purpose of their Facebook presence is simple - to draw more users to their website.

For that purpose, Upwork's Facebook's ads are mostly formatted to drive more website traffic. These ads work pretty much the same way that the previous ads do, with the exception of using a Learn More CTA that brings Facebook users to their website upon clicking.

7.4 Defining and Understanding your Audience

Facebook comprises of over two billion active users who visit the platform daily, but they are not all your target population. As such, your target capabilities should solely focus on your audience, who are your potential clients. Facebook captures and records massive data about their users, including age, gender, location, education, interests, language, and behavior, among others. With such a large population, your target audiences are the crucial elements of your campaign.

Fortunately, the Facebook business manager offers the best filters to acquire your specific audience intended for your information. Some of the ways used to receive a new audience include lookalike, custom, and core audiences. Lookalike audiences are individuals generated from the existing audience as they possess similar features. Core audiences are obtained through setting your criteria manually and filtering the general population within

Facebook. Custom audiences are created from your list of Facebook friends and contact lists as well as from former and current customers.

Lookalike feature of acquiring new audiences is one of the best as it primarily targets users with similar qualities to your existing audience. When creating a lookalike audience, you either choose your filters and criteria or select your preferences and Facebook create your audience automatically. More so, lookalike audiences play a significant role in expanding your market from your existing population to a broader range and equipped with similar features. According to Facebook, it is essential to upload a contact list of between one thousand and fifty thousand to guarantee the quality of your ads.

7.5 Profit from remarketing on Facebook

Gain followers with Facebook Remarketing Lists

The number of likes on your page goes a long way to show how well your Facebook Marketing campaign is doing. Typically, people will not be as impressed by a page that merely has a few hundred likes. It only shows your audience that there isn't too much happening on your page. As you are pushing for more likes, it is, however, of utmost importance for you to get these likes organically. It is a quite dangerous practice to buy followers on Facebook. This is because you need followers who are genuinely interested in the things your page has to offer. This for engagement purposes which ultimately, will drive in more conversions (see next chapter). It may be difficult to grow your followers organically but at the end, there is a gain for every bit of stress you may be put through so this is definitely worth it. The good news is that Facebook allows you to run paid campaigns with the goal of getting page promotions.

Remarketing is a great way to get new likes on your page through promoted content. This is owing to the fact that this promoted content is targeted to reach your most enthusiastic fans to give you more engagement rates which will give you higher relevance scores, organic visibility, and cheaper clicks.

Facebook's Relevance Score metric dictates the amount you spend and the frequency at which your ads are shown to your target audience. The highest influencer of this metric is your engagement rate which is more likely to be higher if your ads are shown through remarketing to those that have already interacted with your brand in one way or the other. They are considered your brand's most loyal customers. This set of people can be described as your brand ambassadors because they are more likely to interact with all your posts and this will increase your relevance score. This will get you cheaper clicks and more visibility. There is also another advantage to this: using sponsored ads to remarket to your loyal followers will also get you more organic visibility. This is how: when one of your Facebook followers likes your post, that post will automatically appear on the timeline of the person's network of friends. This means that there is a potential of some people from this network of friends liking your page so the more your fans are able to see your posts to like it, the more their friends have the potential of liking your page, hence, more organic likes.

Remarket to those that are Already Following your Page

After gaining followers, you have to make sure that these followers are responsive by interacting with your page. The first tip above can be extended by remarketing to those same people who brought in more followers for you and to those that were converted, to also bring in more followers with the help of boosted posts. This tip is bound to work in your favor as it is already tested. The logic is simple; you are remarketing to those that have already interacted with your brand on the Facebook platform. Any user that has taken the step to like your page has certainly achieved a level of loyalty for your brand. This will translate to more engagement from them, which of course, will mean higher relevance scores and more organic reach.

Use Facebook Targeting Options to Layer your Custom Audiences

The number of people of different categories you can reach with Facebook's targeting options is simply mind-blowing. From the girl-next-door to the president of a first-world country, once you have a good knowledge of your audience, finding them wouldn't be a problem. Even though it is very important not to get too granular and limit your reach, it is of more importance to not overstretch your budget through a large arena of Facebook users as this will give great limits to your visibility and lead to lower relevance scores, fewer conversion rates, and even lower returns on investment.

For instance, if you are retargeting a very large audience that runs on the large side, let's say you have over a thousand contacts to remarket to, with only $150 to spare. Instead of sharing your funds in tiny sections, it will be of more effect if you combine every section of your list into a larger group, using demographic targeting to get the most valuable audience that has prospects of conversion at the end.

It is important to balance between your budgets and audience size, but it is also very important to use the layering targeting options at the top of your custom audiences to carry out experiments. This will most likely increase the relevance of your page and make sure your budget is allocated to those audiences that will most likely convert. This will certainly ensure that your resources don't fall on dry land, without yielding fruits.

Keep your Goals in Mind when Scheduling your Ads

When setting up your ads, be very careful to not bore your remarketing audience or fatigue them. Be more aggressive, however, with special offers and in cases where you have longer buying circles. Usually, the life span of Facebook ads are short-lived but instead of running your ads continuously until you run out of the budget, think of the goal you want to achieve with the ads. For example, if you are running ads for Christmas sales or special discounted offers on a particular product, run the ads aggressively for the time when the discounts or sales will be on, without running frequency caps to an audience that wouldn't convert. If on the other hand, the ad is to promote your page to site visitors, this is possibly going to be an ongoing ad set so you can change to schedule to 'from time to time' to keep your ads fresh. Remember, you can schedule your ads to run at a particular time of the day or a particular day of the week. What this means is that you should set your ad schedule with the goal of the ad as a yardstick, to get the best results out of the ad.

Use Lookalike Customers to Layer new Customers into your Custom Audience

This is a way of expanding your audience by duplicating your existing audience to get to an entirely new set of leads. This is a very strong tactic which you can use to expand your reach while finding a new, untapped audience. This is simple - this particular audience may have already converted by patronizing your brand, but you are out in search of new opportunities. What you do is to simply clone your existing in-market retargeting audience. To do this, layer lookalike audiences from the top of your custom audience. Once done, Facebook will help you find leads with similar makeup, who are very likely to be interested in the things you have to offer.

Take Advantage of the Window of Opportunity

By now, you are no longer oblivious of the fact that is not everyone who visits your landing page converts on their first visit. Now, when a person visits your page and bounces almost immediately, it is your responsibility to find out the best time which you can help them make up their minds to interact with you. Let's say, for instance, you run a beauty parlor and a person visits your page but leaves without converting. This means that the person is probably looking for a place to do her hair. Also, chances are that this same person eventually found another option and went with it. Do not take her as a lost customer, this person may still end up being your most loyal customer if you handle the relationship well. Keeping in mind that from the first visit you have already formed a relationship with her, so you are to start timing her from that time. Since she has just gotten her hair done, this means that in the next three months, she will already be in search of other options to get her hair done again because she will want to get it done again. The space between the second and third months is, however, your window of opportunity. This is the time you are expected to aggressively push in retargeting ads to her, to compel her to choose you as not just her one-time place to get her hair done, but as her one-stop shop for all her hair needs and eventually, all her beauty requirements.

To do this, there are two things you can do. First, you can create an ad and target it to all customers that have not visited your site for the past 14 days. This is a very easy option but it may not give us explicit results as the second option, which is to create two audiences: first, an audience of those that visited your site in the past 3 months and the second, an audience of those that have visited in the past 2 months. The window of opportunity for the customer you are trying to target will be in the second option while exempting the first option.

In a nutshell, Facebook remarketing should be one of the focal points of your Facebook ad campaign. The gains of this marketing strategy cannot be emphasized enough as it leads you to achieve some of the major goals of your marketing campaign, with conversion as an ultimate goal. Remember, getting ample returns on investment is very important and this can only happen when your leads convert. It is for this reason that you have to focus on convincing people who already know your brand to patronize you, by remarketing to them.

Chapter 8: Facebook Algorithm

Facebook is a busy place. Most users have a few hundred 'friends', 'like' many pages and are members of a number of groups.

Your news feed is made up of:

- Updates from your 'friends'
- Updates from pages you have liked
- Updates from groups you have joined
- Posts that your friends have shared
- Facebook Ad posts.

A complex algorithm called 'Edgerank' controls what you see on Facebook. Facebook is such a busy platform that without this algorithm your user experience wouldn't be so positive. Imagine that this algorithm is acting like a newspaper editor. The editor's role is to sift through all the news items and make a call on what will be published. Only the most newsworthy stories get published. Edgerank is doing the same on Facebook. Every Facebook user's news feed is individual to them. Facebook knows what you are interested in based on your activity; what you 'like', 'comment on', 'share' and 'click'. If you regularly interact with a page because you find their content interesting, you will find that their posts tend to appear in your news feed. On the other hand, if you have liked pages in the past and have not interacted with their posts you will see their posts less frequently and perhaps not at all.

Your challenge as managers of Facebook pages is to produce content that your audience (the people who like your page) engages with. You need your audience to 'like', 'comment on', 'share' or 'click' on your posts to ensure they continue to see them.

Who Sees Your Posts and Why?

Once you set up a page your first challenge is to get people to 'like' or 'follow' your page. People who 'like' your page automatically become 'followers'. This means they are counted as a page 'like' and may see the posts published on your page in their news feed. People can choose to 'follow' your page but not 'like' it. In this scenario they may see your page posts but are not counted as a page 'like'. Fans of your page can unfollow your page but remain as a page 'like'. This means they are counted as a page like but will not see your content very often.

So if you have a page with 100 followers, when you post on your page you have the potential to reach this audience. If you have 1,000 followers you have the potential to reach 10 times more people. If any of your page likes should share your post you have potential to reach beyond your page likes audience, as your post will appear in the news feed of anyone who has shared your post, therefore reaching their friends.

But just because someone has 'followed' your page does not mean they are guaranteed to see your posts. They will only see your posts if Facebook believes they are interested in your content. Facebook's algorithm, Edgerank, decides whether or not your posts are seen in the news feeds of your page followers.

Although Facebook is constantly tweaking Edgerank, there are some basic factors which determine whether or not your fans see your posts:

How often your fans interact with the posts you publish on your page.

How popular a post is in general. If you publish a post and your fans start engaging with it immediately (liking, commenting, sharing, viewing or clicking), Facebook knows the content is good and is more likely to show it to more people. In this case fans who haven't seen your posts in a while may be reached. Posts that achieve high engagement levels quickly tend to stay longer in the news feed.

The algorithm prioritises posts of friends and family in the news feed.

Chapter 9: How to Monitoring your Facebook Result

Monitoring your performance is important in measuring the effectivity of your advertisements. However, monitoring is not enough since it is needed to be analyzed after. Monitoring and analyzing are two different things. In fact, monitoring only involves seeing the data and its performance but analyzing requires a study and comparison of the collected data given. You must also remember that not all data will be relevant to your campaign, which is why analyzing the data is vital. In fact, this reason justifies why some businesses hire an account analyst for the measurement of their ad results. However, as long as you know the math, you can do it by yourself.

Reading Metrics

Like most websites Facebook collects data about its users. All your communications, personal data and activity is saved by Facebook and used for their own marketing efforts. Unlike other websites, Facebook provides certain data to its users to help their marketing campaigns, free of charge. Though paid ads offer premium tracking features, the metrics offered by Insights are just as powerful if you know how to analyze the data it gives you.

Though you should always be experimenting with new types of posts and promotions, the metrics offered by the Insights feature (located on your business page just below the Facebook search bar) presents graphs representing different activity happening on your page and resulting from your content that gives a tangible measure to how effective your efforts are within different time frames. Let's briefly go over each metric used and how it's presented.

- OVERVIEW

    This is the first page that you'll be taken to when clicking on Insights. It's a brief summary of the metrics that Insight has access to; Overview lists these in tiles but keep in mind that on each Insight page each metric is also listed in a column on the left. The overview tabs show simple graphs. To get more detail about the information measured, click the corresponding tile or subject in the left hand column. Note too that each tile has a stylized "I" in the corner that will display a brief explanation of the metric when hovered over.

- **LIKES**

    Shows when and where your business page was liked. Good for showing how often your page was liked in a certain time frame, which you can correspond with efforts you've employed within said time frame.

- **REACH**

    Shows how many users saw your page and content. Very useful because it breaks down how many likes, comments and shares your posts have received. Also shows what actions users take on your post, including clicking on links, images and videos, as well as negative actions such as hiding, unliking or reporting as spam. If you decide to get into paid advertising through Facebook's ad program this metric also differentiates between reach resulting from paid promotion and reach resulting from organic posts.

- **PAGE VIEWS**

    Breaks down who saw what parts of your business page based on demographics like age and location. Can be used to observe where specific groups are traveling to, allowing you assess their needs or improve your page design and traffic control efforts.

- **ACTIONS ON PAGE**

    Shows who clicked an action on your page and how often. Despite the name this isn't limited to just your Call To Action button. It also includes clicking on different tabs and hyperlinks related to contact and personal information.

- **POSTS**

    This serves two important functions. The first shows how many people responded to posts by reach, clicks (on hyperlinks, hashtags, videos and images) as well as reactions, comments and shares. The second shows when these things happens and associates them with demographics, giving you insight onto which groups of your customers are online when.

- **EVENTS**

    If you host an event as part of your marketing campaign (using Facebook's Event function), this metric will keep track of its reach, how people engaged with it, tickets sold (if any) and the demographics of those who responded to it in someway and how they responded.

- **VIDEOS**

    Breaks down how much of your videos were watched, dividing the results into two categories: which videos were watched for three or more seconds and how many were watched for ten or more seconds. A third option tells you which of your videos were the most successful.

- **CONVERSATIONS**

    Finally, this section keeps tally of how many conversations you were involved in (as in, actively participating in) during the given time frame.

Much of this data is displayed in simple graph formats. To get more or less data, you can choose to adjust the time frame for which you want the data.

By carefully analyzing the data Insight collects you can see what parts of your marketing campaign work and which ones need help or should be abandoned. You can also better determine which posts are of high quality based on customer reactions to them. Repeat your successes and tweak your failures according to the guideline laid out by the data Insights collects.

Chapter 10: Facebook Ads and Gdpr compliance

AdWords vs. Facebook

This is a question that often inexperienced marketers ask. The answer is always "it depends".

We need to understand what are the goals that we want to achieve with our advertising campaign. It is often fundamental to combine both strategies. It all depends on the type of question: whether this is latent or conscious (or both).

If the goal is to make branding and then stimulate users who do not know us and may be interested (latent demand), the best choice is Facebook Ads, which will allow you, as we will see later, to reach potential customers. You can do this with various types of targeted campaigns and get leads.

Similarly, you can also take advantage of ads on the Google Display Network to reach potential customers by submitting your banners to specific placements.

If users are already looking for your product or service, the right approach is to use Google AdWords by creating ads on the Search Network. In this case, the user is already in a much lower part of the funnel, therefore more inclined to purchase as the user is looking for your product/service.

Obviously, in most cases, we will find both types of demand and we will have to work on both platforms jointly.

The key is to understand where the user is inside our sales funnel and act accordingly; we will never tire of stressing it.

Going inside, it will be useful to retarget users who have shown interest in the product or service working with both Facebook Ads and AdWords through ads on the display network.

What if we intercept potential customers on Facebook through FB Ads and these, then, look for us on Google but we are not positioned in an organic way (without paying) for that keyword?

Simple. They will click on a competition link. The risk is, therefore, to practically advertise competitors. Understand well then how important it is, in the absence of organic positioning with SEO, that we must also have Google ads on the search network to cover some keywords as well.

Facebook marketing is not so powerful if done alone; it is something that some people see as a disadvantage.

Each Facebook campaign consists of 3 levels and it starts from the campaign level, which consists of one or more ad groups.

 As you have just read, for each campaign you create, you will have to choose a goal. This is the real distinctive factor at the campaign level.

At the Ad Group level (Ad Set), you will have to choose the target, the available budget, the publication times, the offer, and the placements.

Going down the hierarchy, at the level of the announcements, you can set the type of announcement (image, video, carousel, etc.), all the texts, the call to action (action button), and the destination links.

As mentioned, the structure is hierarchical, so if you pause (or delete) for example a group of ads, the same thing will happen to all ads below that group.

The Definition of the Goals

Now that we understand the structure of a Facebook campaign and what are the parameters to be set for each level, we are ready to launch our first campaign.

The first question is: "What is the goal to be achieved?"
Do you want to sell a certain product because maybe you have an e-commerce store? Do you want to create awareness or reputation? Do you want to have leads?
Often, in a complete web marketing strategy, we will have to create different campaigns for the different phases of the purchasing process. We can then create different ads depending on whether the target user does not know our brand or knows it but does not know our product/service, or, for example, knows our product/service and may be interested in a commercial offer.
Facebook itself in the creation phase will propose you different objectives divided into 4 macro-categories.
Let's see them in detail one by one.

- **BRAND AWARENESS**

When to use it: in large-scale campaigns, when there is not a particular action that you want to take to the user. This goal will be more attractive to large companies that can afford to launch campaigns for pure branding. For smaller companies, however, almost every other objective will give better and more significant results.

- **REACH**

When to use it: similar to the brand awareness goal, the reach objective is functional to reach the maximum number of users to which the ad will show. With the introduction of the rules, Facebook now allows you to put a cap on the frequency with which the ad is shown to the same user; in this sense, the goal for reach becomes very useful when you have to work with a relatively small audience and you want everyone to view the ad.

- **TRAFFIC**

When to use it: when we want to take users to a website, or on a landing page, for example. It is a very interesting goal when promoting content, such as a blog post.

- **LEADS**

When to use it: the lead ads greatly simplify the signup process from mobile devices. When someone clicks on the ad, a form opens with all personal contact information already pre-filled based on the information they share on Facebook, such as name, surname, phone, and email address. This aspect makes the process really fast and within 2 clicks, one to open the ad and one to send the information.

The only problem with this type of objective is that, often, the email address used to sign up for Facebook several years ago is obsolete and has not been updated for too long. In this case, we would get a useless contact. As a result, it has been seen that better conversion campaigns perform that point to specific external landing pages with data to be filled out.

Another aspect to keep in mind is that lead ads do not allow you to include all the information you want in the offer, like on a landing page. Therefore, for campaigns that require a great deal of cognitive attention from the user, a campaign for conversions will be more successful.

That said, in any case, it is always better to do a test between the two approaches and see which performs better, because each case and sector can behave differently. The success of a Facebook campaign depends almost entirely on how we select the right target. Good results are not obtained by trying to guess the interests, but only by experimenting and testing, and knowing the right tools.

- ## THE PIXEL OF FACEBOOK

James Fend, a Facebook expert, is categorical: the pixel of Facebook should always be installed anyway, even if at the moment, we are not interested in campaigning and even if we believe we do not need anything. But why? Because when it is installed (by entering a code on our website), it starts recording data. The pixel will then be able to make us reach users who come into contact with our site, and these users can be used in future for our listings. It must be installed "regardless" because we may regret not having collected the data when these will help us.

- **SPY ON COMPETITORS' SPONSORSHIPS**

Coming into an advertisement published by our competitors can be a golden opportunity: we can "spy" the target they have chosen for their sponsorship. Just click on "Why do I view this ad?", where the magic is accomplished: we will see exactly what target has set our competitor.
If the interests that our competitor has selected work we do not know, we can get an idea based on the vanity metrics. And in any case, we now have some tools to test.

- **CREATE A PERSONALIZED AUDIENCE**

Facebook gives us many options to intercept our potential customers and we should always start from our customers or our traffic. For example, we can upload a file with our LinkedIn contacts or newsletter subscribers. We can take advantage of the pixel and select who visits specific pages of the site or generate events (such as sales or add to cart), who spends more time on the site or who visit him more often, or who opens the newsletter.

- **TAKE ADVANTAGE OF OTHER CHANNELS, LIKE ADWORDS**

The ads on Facebook certainly do not answer to any conscious question: we launch the bait to a potentially interested public and hope that someone will realize that they need our product or service. With ads on AdWords instead, we intercept the conscious need: the user need the tires and search on Google, find our ad, and land on our site.
Well, we can take advantage of the results obtained from AdWords. Such as? Just leave the pixel of Facebook "listening" and with the data obtained create our custom audience based on traffic on the site.

At that point the user, who has seen our model X of tires but who has not completed the purchase, will see "chased" from our product even within Facebook.

- **USE A/B TESTING**

The analysis of the results obtained must always be exploited to our advantage. Facebook gives us the opportunity with A/B testing.

Facebook Leads: How to Get Quality Leads

Do not stop at the lead. Look for the quality of the contact. Landing pages generate higher quality contacts because they intercept the aware questions and require the commitment to fill out the forms, and the quality is paid (with CPL, costs per lead, high).
The Facebook lead ads have unparalleled CPLs, but the quality is affected. The Facebook form is pre-filled with the user's data and often the latter submits without giving weight to the action, perhaps even just out of curiosity. That's why with the ads, you should never use insertions and forms that are too simple.
Indeed, complex forms, in which we challenge the user with questions (or even propose a quiz) can have a considerable engagement.
Among the various platforms in which to start implementing social media marketing activities, Facebook tends to be one that best meets the marketing objectives of a company.
Numbers are important, but not all count in the same way.

The data have no value in itself; they only have it if they are functional to trigger processes of understanding and improvement of our actions. When it comes to analyzing the activities undertaken on social networks and making reports to understand how it is going, between Internal Insights and External Tools, the feeling is sometimes to get lost in counting and not being able to get some useful information to act better. Today, we see which values should be kept under control with the Insights that Facebook gives us for free.
So let's go to the point.
What are the most important Facebook Insight metrics? Obviously, it depends. It depends on the objectives and KPIs we have set ourselves.

GDPR Compliance

The General Data Protection Regulation or GDPR is a regulation on an individual's personal data that came into the picture in mid-2018 and has had an impact on affiliate marketing. When this regulation came into play, many types of campaigns and tactics became redundant overnight and caused affiliate marketers to rethink their strategies. With the growing awareness of privacy data, you as an affiliate marketer will need to ensure that your website won't increase your visitor's privacy fears. For this reason, a Secure Sockets Layer or SSL needs to be used to create an environment where potential customers feel safe when making purchases and sharing their personal data.

 GDPR is the 'elephant in the room' when it comes to any type of marketing that involves cookies. Cookies require a website to collect personal information from visitors, often without them being explicitly aware. Unfortunately, that directly flies in the face of the General Data Protection Regulation and ePrivacy Directive set up by the EU.

In other words, it's now illegal to track users or collect their data without explicitly saying so. This is not an unsurmountable challenge – in fact it is easily remedied by adding a notice to your website. With that said though, it's very important that you do this, in order to ensure you are in compliance with the law.

Redundant Ads – Another issue is that you might end up retargeting to people who have already bought your product. This is now the most redundant and least targeted form of ad imaginable! We're not talking about retargeting with new products, but rather retargeting **the precise same product**.

That's why it can be a good idea to also **exclude** some people from your lists – such as if they actually land on the 'Thank You' page. Another fortunate saving grace is that most people won't click on ads for things they just bought – meaning that you won't actually pay for them. So it's not as much of a waste as it might at first seem.

Mistaken Identities – As a professional writer, I am often tasked with writing about products for resellers. Thus, I spend a lot of time looking at store listings for things I have no interest in buying. The bad news? That means I get all **kinds** of strange adverts.

Likewise, you've no doubt at some point bought something for a family member or friend only to have that item repeatedly shoved in your face for weeks afterward wherever you go online.

Occasionally this can happen, but the good news is that once again, it shouldn't cost you as long as no one actually clicks those ads. What's more, is that you can use other filters (such as demographics) to reduce the likelihood of this happening.

CONCLUSION

It has been a wonderful journey taking you through everything you need to know about Facebook Marketing to earn you conversions. Certainly, there are best industry practices and there are some not-so-popular ones that are capable of working magic for you, we hope you have been able to grasp it all.

The essence of this book is to make sure Facebook Marketers grasp proper knowledge of the best ways to go about their Facebook marketing journey. From the first chapter to the last, we have made a conscious effort to take you through every step you need to take in this interesting, albeit complicated, journey of marketing with the Facebook platform. From the beginning of your Facebook Marketing campaign, which starts with you creating a Facebook page, to knowing your way around Facebook Business manager, to Facebook Insights, which is the home of every activity that takes place on your Facebook page, this is a one-of-a-kind book that lets you digest everything about marketing on the world's largest online community. Facebook advertising seems like unknown territory to many marketers who feel as though they don't know their way around creating ads and managing them. Well, we hope that after reading this eBook, you will become a master in advertising.

All the strategies contained in this book are tested and trusted and are not merely author recommendations so it is a complete package of reliable ways to get your returns on investments while making sure that you do not incur unnecessary expenses for your ad campaigns. We have broken down all the intricacies of Facebook's great targeting options.

Although there are over 1.5 billion active users on the platform daily, Facebook has made it clear that they are focused on connecting users so businesses have to invest their time and money forget a chance to be among the top players in their respective fields. While you can avoid spending all your time on your Facebook Marketing campaign with automation options, you will have to be ready to put in financial resources to get yourself out there by paying for ads and sponsored posts. These are very important points in your campaign. Despite the fact that Facebook has every category of people that you need for your business, you may fail to make the best out of these numbers if you do not stick to the rules.

Finally, strategies, skills, tips, and tricks for Facebook Marketing are available to everyone who seeks to gain knowledge about it. This means that your competitors are also in search of ways to improve themselves to be the best in their industry. For everyone who seeks this knowledge, there is an ample amount of it waiting for them. You need to stay creative and unique with every strategy you choose to adopt. Above all, be convincing, for this is the only way your customer will choose you above your competition. Good luck!

*Did this book help you in some way?
If so, I'd love to hear about it.

Honest reviews help readers find the
right book for their needs."*

www.ingramcontent.com/pod-product-compliance
Lightning Source LLC
Chambersburg PA
CBHW071419210526
45465CB00001B/453